Home in Ethiopia

~ An Oklahoma Family Story ~

Arlene Thies

WJB Publishing, Bill Boudreau
www.billboudreau.com

To my daughter, LeAnn Thies Storck, who was not with us in Ethiopia.
And, to my two outstanding grandchildren — Jennifer and Alex Carr

Tom & Marilyn —
I hope you enjoy
this ride with me —
+ I was not wearing
a purple shirt in
those days.
Arlene Thies

Ethiopia Emperor, Haile Selassie – 1930 - 1974

Acknowledgements

Marilyn Coulson, a friend, introduced me to Bill Boudreau, a writer. Without her, *Home in Ethiopia* would never have happened.

Lynette Thies, my daughter, transported my 1960's photos from a blurry past to a colorful present.

Bill Boudreau encouraged me to take the story out of a drawer. A special "thank you" to Bill for all his help with proof reading, picture enhancements, formatting, cover design, and everything else required to make this book a reality.

Oklahoma Contract with Oklahoma State University provided the opportunity and support to live and work in Africa, the experience of a lifetime.

Ethiopian Proverb: A house can't be built for the rainy season that is past.

Prelude

The fourth quarter my of life is filled with memories and leaves no space for what-ifs. It's a time to count my blessings and cherish events of my past. At home alone with the quiet, listening to good music, it's a time to remember those special moments and reminisce the year of 1961.

Did we really sit together drinking tea from those little German-made teacups, under the grape arbor while watching sailboats on a crater lake in Ethiopia? Many years ago it was a reality for me, my three small children, and a husband wrapped up in his work.

Looking at a map of Africa, in geographic distance it's far, far away. But not in my mind!

Haile Selassie was the emperor at that time, a small man in stature, only five-foot two but big on the world stage. Being a direct descendant of the Queen of Sheba and referred to as the Lion of Judah, he remains a symbol of strength and reserved for a person of royalty. His reign began in 1930.

In 1936, prior to WWII, the Italians came, overpowered the Emperor, and took over the country. During that time, he and his family lived in Europe. By 1942 Haile Selassie thought it time to return to his country. He came from the north country, reconquered Addis Ababa, and was back in power.

The culture, customs, celebrations, food, everything was special. Haile Selassie wanted better conditions for his people. He and his family worked at improving the country, however the people lived under impoverished conditions. The Emperor wanted to improve education and the way of life. The Ethiopian people are beautiful with refined physical features, and support strong religious and cultural traditions.

Amheric is the most common language. I still try to remember my limited repertoire. My favorite word was boiled eggs — *yetakakalal inkalal*. It is as much fun to say as dirty dog — *kashasha wooshaw*. These words are spelled according to sounds I remember. Of course, I know *tanastalin, indeminalu* which is "Hello, how are you?" That is about the most I remember, other than counting. Lots of fun words and sounds. Two phrases have stuck with me and I still use them today. Since you really couldn't knock on the door of a tukel (house), you just came to the door and called out *"hode."* The answer to it was *"cariboo."* Love the words *"gid yellum"* which means, "It just really doesn't make any difference." That was a frequently used expression and has remained with me throughout the years.

Rain on the roof: Our house was built of brick with corrugated tin roof and no insulation of any kind. Just don't count on any communication when the rain came. At times, we had extreme rains. It was either a rainy season or dry season, no four seasons. Poinsettias bloomed in December.

Never had tasted lasagna like we ate at the Addis airport restaurant. Sometimes we went there after mission church and eat typical Italian food. I always ordered baked lasagna topped with a meat sauce before having filet mignon.

Trips to the lakes and Jima were special times. Going with different friends, I have many fond memories. Sometimes fishing, sometimes hunting, and sometimes just to get away and enjoy the scenes and encountered many people along the way. Not able to talk with them due to the variety of languages. Each tribe had its own language, or dialect.

That new experience was life changing. It certainly made me more compassionate and thinking of others in need. There was much joy and laughter among the people even when they had so little. We had so much.

Americans became friends and family quickly. We needed one another and we were there for each other. It was always pay it forward. Our purpose in going to Ethiopia was to assist them in their daily living and sometimes we were the ones in need.

I had a busy 1992 when I decided to write about my special two and one-half years in Ethiopia. Using an old junky piece of a computer, I struggled with writing that lasted for a month or more. Apparently, I had more important things to do and the pages were put in a folder, and tucked in a drawer.

Now it is 2017 and much of this was written in 1992 but we lived it in 1961 through 1963. How quickly the years go by and so much change takes place.

Come ride with me as we come back from Addis to Debra Zeit. The sights, sounds, and aromas I still remember: At home in Debra Zeit and trips to the lakes. Then enjoy the many pictures and keep in mind that this happened more than fifty years ago.

The pictures come from slides stored in a book many years ago. I brought them out, my daughter, Lynette, scanned them into the computer. No such thing as a digital camera!

At that time, 50-years ago, I did not have a tape recorder to record the wonderful music and sounds. I did not have a telephone or a newspaper. Would have been great to phone a friend. Sometimes I just wished for a piece of store bought fluffy white American made bread.

But, I still remember.

Ethiopia

On a day in the early 1960s, the beauty of Montana was in full display—the trees and mountains were spectacular. Although in winters, temperature dropped as low as 40 degrees below zero. It was hard to realize the extreme cold on that day. The sun shone, blue sky, calm, and still. Being out on a day like that for the first five or ten minutes was wonderful until the cold struck. Frostbite came quick. Cars needed to be garaged with a head-bolt heater, otherwise impossible to get it started. Driving was strange. Tires felt and sounded like blocks of wood thumping along on the snow and ice packed streets. Streets piled high, plows constantly on the move clearing the snow.

Traveling the mountain passes, with heavy snow falling, traffic moving slowly, was hazardous. Slipping off the road could mean a long slide down the mountain; however, roads were not as slippery as in Oklahoma. Extreme cold does not permit melting—it was hard, packed solid.

Sundays, after Thanksgiving, we always made a trip to the Bridger Mountains, which is on the way to Yellowstone Park, to cut a Christmas tree. That was my favorite day of the year. Zeke, my husband, would stay at the bottom so I could go up with our friends and find that perfect tree. It was always an easy slide back down the mountain and such a good feeling.

Chili never tasted so good when we got back to the home of the Browns. Mrs. Brown always made the chili, I made the pies, and Helen Eslick and Elenore Niffenegar brought the extras.

Montana was gorgeous in the winter and the "two weeks" of summer were fabulous. Excellent trout fishing in the many streams, if the trouts were bigger than the mosquitoes! It's really God's country. Also, a gardener's dream as long as the season was long enough for some vegetables. I really enjoyed the flowers and garden. It never got so hot in the summer that it burned everything up like it did in Oklahoma. We only had to worry about the frost coming too soon.

Our house, a shoebox on stilts, had two bedrooms and a full basement. We rented the downstairs. We'd moved into that house shortly before Lynette was born.

We lived in Bozeman, Zeke was employed at Montana State College.

I was mother of the household. Lynette, my youngest at that time, seven months old, otherwise known as Sissy, but to me she was really "Soppy Sara." She was born June 13, 1960. She was about five months old. Monte "Drippy Gus," the second oldest, was two on September 25, and Steve, the eldest, "Wet Pants Benny," was four in April.

We had decided to stay in Montana for a while. Zeke had applied for various positions and nothing materialized. He wanted to join the Oklahoma team from Stillwater to assist in agriculture in Ethiopia. At the time he applied, all positions were filled. Since we had heard nothing more, we kind of forgot about it. There was also a position at Purdue University that he had applied for but they wanted someone with a PhD. A few months later, we received a letter that they would reconsider a position if he was still interested as they could not fill the position with a degreed individual. By that time it was too late. We were already committed. Since things were not working out, we added a brick planter to the front of the house, and put on new storm doors and decided to stay for a while.

And then it happened! Mr. William Abbott from Agriculture and Mechanical College (now known as Oklahoma State University) wanted to schedule an appointment for the following week to interview the whole Thies family for an assignment in Ethiopia. A&M had a contract with the United States government and the Ethiopian government to send an agriculturalist to Ethiopia to assist them with agricultural training of the farmers. This was referred to as the Point Four Program and had been in effect for six or eight years already. A&M had American staff at the college in Alameya near Harar, a high school in Jimma, an experimental station in Bishoftu, and management located in Addis Ababa, the capital. Zeke was being considered for the manager position at the experimental station.

Waiting the arrival of Mr. Abbott, tension ran high. We knew what our decision would be if Zeke were offered the position. Mr. Abbott arrived on Tuesday of the following week and spent the full day with us filling us in on the details of the job, but mostly we talked about living conditions and what life would be like in Africa. Zeke would work in Debra Zeit and we could live in Addis, the capital and largest city. Mr. Abbott had been over there several times. He was very familiar with the conditions. The name Bishoftu had recently been changed to Debra Zeit to give it a more flattering name. Debra Zeit means "Hill of Olives" while Bishoftu meant "stinking fish." It is a small village located about thirty kilometers or fifty miles to the southeast of Addis. Addis is located on a very high plateau, an elevation close to ten thousand feet making it rather a cool climate even though it was near the equator. Situated several thousand feet lower in altitude, Debra Zeit was considerably warmer. Temperature would be mild but not tropical. We would have rainy and dry seasons with Addis having heavier rain.

After a day of talking about details, Mr. Abbott offered Zeke the job and we accepted immediately. We could not pass up the opportunity. We were both intrigued by the thought of living in a foreign country, especially Africa. While in grade school, I had read quite a few books on Africa and was totally fascinated by the stories of the game hunts and primitive living. I remembered the books by Oza Johnson who lived and traveled there in the early 1900s. We were disturbed about how it would affect the kids. Medical facilities were going to be our biggest problem. We knew there were families over there. We were assured that the facilities were adequate unless one had a serious problem. In that event, they would pay the airfare to the United States.

We had about two months to prepare for the trip. They wanted us there early in January 1961. We would visit family in Oklahoma over Christmas holiday. Zeke would take a leave of absence from Montana State for two years and hopefully he would be able to return. We would put our furniture, etc. in storage and had planned to lease the house. Response from friends was mixed. Some thought we were completely out of our minds, taking three little kids into the unknown. Others thought it an exciting thing to do. That was the best time. Easier to travel before the kids reached school age. Anyway, the decision was made. We were going!

Limited time, we had two pressing things to attend to—obtain birth certificates for passports. Zeke's presented a problem, they couldn't locate him in New Orleans' registry. After several persistent phone calls, they found it. We obtained the necessary passports and visas. All of that required a few weeks to accomplish. We needed to obtain eight different immunity shots, some required a series of two or three. Dr. Heetricks worked out a schedule. We got them all during the allotted time, scheduled them in such a way to keep the after effects to a minimum. Steve was always the sickest before. He had anxiety attacks and invariably had to "pitch cookies." After the second week, the doctor gave us a tranquilizer for him but he still seemed to be bothered. We always had a certain amount of problems the day of the shots, or the next day—irritability, temperature, and sometimes just plain sick. Monte seemed to suffer most from the after effects. Sissy also needed the smallpox shot and the doctor gave it to her just before we left Bozeman. That really proved to be a problem. Her arm became very, very red, and sore. We all had our last shots in Oklahoma City, which was for yellow fever. It was only available in large cities, or the capital city of the state. Easier than getting it in Montana, we got the shots on the 23rd of December and had planned to be in Oklahoma for Christmas. Without a doubt, the most difficult part of it all was getting all those shots and felt we could not tolerate one more.

We were allowed 600 pounds, air freight, and about 2000 pounds sea freight. We borrowed some money and did a lot of shopping, as suggested, take clothes and shoes for two years. However, we would have APO (Army Post Office) privilege which would be a real plus. The U.S. Air Force had a base in Addis and Asmara, north on the Ethiopian border. We would also have commissary privilege, access to American canned and packaged food. Cheap liquor was the best bargain at the commissary.

My sewing machine proved to be the greatest asset as it not only took care of a necessity, I made clothes for all of us, and provided lots of hours of entertainment for me. I had taken along fabric and knew I would be able to obtain more from the states through APO privilege.

After several shopping sprees, the time came to get organized for the packing. Oklahoma Contract would pay for the packing of the sea freight, but I needed to do the rest. The hardest part was deciding which stack to put it in while sorting. The packers would be in for one day. Everything needed to be ready for them. They would also pack the items which were to go into storage. That absolutely had to be the most frustrating part of getting ready, and then, I had three little helpers. Not only did I need to determine which stack to put things in and keep the kids from taking it back out. They simply could not understand why their toys and good stuff had to be put in some stack and left there. Sissy was even trying to get in on the act as she was really getting around for her age, and of course we were still having the weekly interruption, the shots which caused all of us to be feisty and irritable. I packed the airfreight earlier than the rest and it consisted of all necessities for our arrival in Addis. Supposedly, it was to be shipped several weeks in advance so it would be there when we got there. A four-week period was considered adequate time.

Somehow, I got it all sorted out. The packers came and did their part. The only large items we took were the freezer and a washing machine to operate on a 220 transformer. We would obtain the transformers over there. Now everything that was left would either go into storage or in our suitcases. They allowed us additional poundage for our luggage. I didn't know if that was good, or bad, as we would be traveling for several weeks with suitcases, bags, and boxes galore. We had to leave a few things. We really didn't know what we needed anyway. At least I didn't get any of the kids in a box or suitcase! We were leaving Montana at Christmas time to go to California, Oklahoma, New York, Athens, with a destination of Africa. That required quite a variation in clothing and meant we would be traveling for about a month. That was before the days of perma-press and disposable diapers. There were plenty of problems with washing, ironing, and Lynette still in diapers and on a bottle. I didn't know if disposable diapers were available or if I just didn't know about them. But we traveled with wet diapers all the way to Africa.

Well, let me tell you, the last couple of days in Bozeman were pretty hectic and I was still throwing things in the last big box as the Fehrers came to get us. Little Joe saw that blue bowling shirt in the box and told his mom "there is that bowling shirt you wanted, Mom," but I didn't even have enough sense to say, "Take it out." Guess I thought I was going to league bowl in Debra Zeit.

The Fehrers had three kids, we had three kids, and we had masses of luggage loaded in their station wagon. They drove us to Billings to catch a flight and I can't recall how we got everything and everybody in that station wagon, but we did. Must have been like some "Ma Kettle" episode, as I don't see how it could have been any other way. Marge and Virg said they could do it and whatever they said they meant. They were two of the best people I have ever known.

We left Billings, Montana, the evening of December 21, 1960, temperature 10 degrees below zero. We boarded a tiny plane so small that we loaded from the back, walking up a ramp. Monte did not like that ramp and he threw a screaming fit and refused to walk up it, so while carrying "Sissy" and other paraphernalia, I had to pull him up the ramp, bawling all the way. That was only the beginning of his disliking height, stairs, escalators, etc. He'd taken a tumble down the basement stairs a few months before the trip and I followed him all the way down to the last stop, grabbing, and reaching, but not able to stop the fall.

Our yellow fever shots were scheduled for the afternoon of the 23rd. We had been told that we would surely be sick from that one. But none of us had any effects. So, on to Alva, Oklahoma, for Christmas. Lynette was really suffering from the smallpox vaccination. She was running a temperature, her arm was red, swollen, hot and shiny. Uncle Herman, in Alva, was really upset. He didn't think we had any business going overseas to start with, and why would anyone do that to a little one. I had my doubts also. We didn't know much about facilities in Ethiopia. We had already put the kids through a lot. I was getting scared!

While in Alva, I called my friend, Norlyne Niehaus Keahey, who had just returned from college in Ethiopia. We would not be living at the college, but at least she would have knowledge of the country. She had been there for two years. Her husband was president of the school and had been there longer. She had married him while he was on a home leave. She gave us a positive picture of everything and said they had a wonderful time while there. She had also had a baby and felt the medical facilities were adequate. Talking to her certainly improved the overall picture and I felt more comfortable.

Zeke and I went to Stillwater for a day of orientation. We left the kids with Grandpa and Grandma—the first time I had been away from them, except to go to the hospital to have another. We stayed with "Pappy" and Mrs. Martin who were very special friends of Zeke's. While he was in college at Oklahoma State, he'd basically worked his way through school. He worked for "Pappy" who oversaw the Entertainment Bureau and traveled around the state putting on programs for benefits, civic groups or anyone else who wanted entertainment. Many times, they would entertain as a good will for the benefit of the college and to recruit students. Zeke sang and played guitar and was especially known for "Onions." "Pappy" and Mrs. Martin treated the students like their own kids and he loved to reminisce and kept up with what was happening to "his kids." We had a memorable evening. Orientation the next day was just a formality. Zeke met with Billy Webb whom he would replace. Billy filled Zeke on what he had been doing.

Then we went to Ponca City. Visited with Fritz and Verna, Roy and Gladys, and families. Stayed in Alva a few days. The children got to know their grandfather and grandmother. Back to Oklahoma City, we stayed with H.G. and Loris and their kids. No matter which household we stayed, we always ended up with plenty of kids, they got introduced to cousins. Loris and H.G. took us to the airport. By that time we were nervous. We bided our last goodbye for two years.

At Will Rogers airport, we boarded the plane at 3:05 p.m., Wednesday, January 4, 1961, and flew to Washington D.C. where we met the Terwilligers. Darlene and Louis lived in Bozeman when he was on the staff at Montana State, and we lived in the faculty housing. They were good friends. They drove us around Washington. It was a beautiful at nighttime. After the drive, they came to the hotel with us. We talked into the wee hours. Next morning, we took the kids for a walk and saw lots of construction work going on in the area, and the next thing we knew, we were entering a side door of the White House. We had crossed Pennsylvania Avenue. Building stands for Kennedy's inauguration were in progress.

We left Washington in the afternoon and flew to New York, and changed to TWA's terminals. We would depart at 7:00 p.m. I can still recall that wait, knowing that we would board a half hour before flight time. Traveling first class, we had ordered our dinners several weeks prior to the flight. The kids would have steak and Zeke and I had ordered lobster.

Everything went according to schedule. We boarded first because we had children. Immediately after takeoff, they started to bring us drinks, and that continued through the night. We had before dinner drinks, during dinner drinks, and after dinner drinks—wine, champagne, brandy, liquors along with all the regulars. For a little gal from Alva, Oklahoma, the experience was extraordinary!

The kids drank ginger ale and had never tasted anything like that before. Then there were the appetizers, including caviar. Monte liked it. He sat in his seat and decided it was better to straddle the arm of the chair, eating caviar and crackers and drinking ginger ale. What a deal! Sissy didn't care about any of that. She was tired and went right to sleep. That was nice. It gave me an opportunity to enjoy the dinner and service. We ate and drank all we could hold. Due to the excitement, the boys couldn't settle down to sleep. When the boys finally fell asleep, Sissy woke up. By the time she went back to sleep, we were only forty-five minutes out of Paris. We landed in Paris for refueling. Since the kids were sleeping, we stayed on the plane and then on to Rome. We flew over the Alps. The scenery was magnificent. I loved the snow and the mountains, but I was tired.

Rome! I shall never forget Rome that first time. While landing, the countryside looked beautiful and green, spacious and inviting. Having seen the Alps with all the snow and mountains, now it looked like springtime with the sun shining, all the green, and I remember a strong feeling of elation, of excitement. It felt wonderful! We taxied into the airport and a different feeling came over me. We were escorted into a musty old terminal. Once inside, the doors were locked behind us. We were going no place. The people were strange, the language was strange, and if you have ever experienced the masses of Italians together in a confined space with everyone babbling at once, you get the picture. I was petrified and I couldn't see the sunshine of the outside world—claustrophobia! That was the oldest, dingiest, mustiest, scariest, frightening place I had ever been, and I needed to go to the bathroom. I wanted to go home! That was just too much.

After a two-hour layover in Rome, we flew to Athens, where we would have several days to rest. That flight was like four hours. We really wanted to sleep but they were serving more drinks and lots of food. Of course, it was lunch time there, but 8:00 a.m. for us. We had had breakfast between Paris and Rome, continental style. Lunch was served in courses, along with a variety of drinks. We were offered cold cuts, soup, and salad, and then the main course followed by pastries, fruit, and cheese, but who wanted to eat! I was feeling more like being sick.

Greece was so different than Rome. Staying in Athens, we needed to go through customs. We were met by a TWA representative who helped us go through customs and get our baggage checked. The kids and I sat in the airport and waited for them to take care of things that needed attention and check on our departure, three days later. We had masses of luggage, boxes, and bags. It occupied a hotel room to store all that. I sat like an old cluck hen protecting her brood when a handsome young Greek man came over and started playing with the kids. Monte took an immediate liking to him and they laughed and had a wonderful time even though neither could understand a word the other had said. I was very apprehensive but tolerated it and later found that the Greek people are just a very friendly people. We took several suitcases to the hotel. The atmosphere in that airport was so different than Rome. I was reasonably comfortable with Athens. The travel agency had a suite of rooms reserved for us in one of the old hotels, the Grande Britagne.

A limousine took us to the hotel. Downtown on the main square, near the palace, bore all the beauty and grandeur of old Europe. The lobby contained beautiful old European furniture, huge chandeliers overhead, lovely carpets. We were in another world and comfortable. The people were friendly, it seemed that everyone wanted to please us, make us feel welcome. Up in our suite of rooms, we settled in for several days. I was exhausted.

Excellent service, both in and out of the room. The maid popped unannounced and did her puttering around. She was pleasant even though she did not speak any English. We nearly ate all our meals in the room. We had a dining room and were forewarned about European dining. They did not have eating establishments where one could get sandwiches and light meals. The hotel dining room served dinner to the children between five and six o'clock. The food consisted of cereal, eggs, and fruits. Children were not permitted in the dining room in the evening when dinner was served to adults. Steve really resented that. He wanted something besides "breakfast" for his dinner. The food was strange, so we ordered as American as possible. The coffee was most unusual. They served it extra strong along with a pot of hot milk. At first, we could not figure out why they brought the hot milk. But they would pour half coffee, half milk, one silver pot in either hand. Bread was always hard crusted and of course the kids didn't like that. Eating was such a different experience for the kids. Dinner was served in elegance with white table cloth, china, silver, and all, even when we were having room service.

Jet lag for adults is a problem but quite something else for kids. They didn't understand what was happening. I found out quick that they weren't going to be bothered by what the sun was doing or not doing. They took an afternoon nap at seven or eight in the evening, and I thought they had gone to bed for the night. Surprise! By midnight they were going strong and having a wonderful time. We played games, read, and watched the celebrations across the way. The Greeks were eating, drinking, and dancing until the wee hours. The kids finally settled down again and we woke up in time to go out the first morning but the second morning we just slept it through and none of us got up till lunch time. We had planned to go on a tour of the city. On an afternoon tour we visited the Acropolis and the Parthenon. The tour took us to an area where one could look down on the city of Athens. We could have enjoyed it more but the bus driver said it was much too far to walk for me while carrying Sissy. I left Sissy with the driver in the bus. Walking away, I did more watching the bus than enjoying the tour. She was still sleeping when we got back. We had intended to take a tour to the palace, changing of the guard, etc, but we ran out of time. Our best pastime was walking. The hotel resided in the center of it all. We walked the square and went shopping—many fur shops, and handwoven fabrics, and clothes, beautiful hand-loomed wool skirts available. I really liked one in fabulous colors, but we were going to a "warm country." Copper items with traditional Greek designs were common. Tourists, and I, liked the many statues made from a marble-type material. We bought several. We discovered they were delicate and easily breakable. We browsed little shops that carried magazines, candies, cigarettes, and a variety of small novelty items. We saw many outdoor places where one could sit next to the street, watch the traffic, and have a cool drink. One could not afford that very often. Orange juice cost $1.00 American. That was expensive at that time. Little was available in bottled drinks.

We enjoyed sitting, watching people, and the noisy traffic. When the stoplight changed to green, the traffic went into motion, along with the blaring horns. Drivers did not sit and wait for the car ahead to start moving, they just moved, and the automobile ahead had better be on its way. I wouldn't have wanted to drive in that traffic!

While walking the streets, people were extremely friendly, greeted with "American, Americano." Some would rub Monte's blonde head. I was amazed he had any hair left. A description of Monte is in order: he was built like his maternal grandfather, short and round. He wore overalls and coveralls. If he wore pants, they always dragged as he couldn't hold them up with that pot tummy, a light complexion, white hair, he never knew a stranger. He loved all the attention. Steve, quite opposite, he was tall and thin, dark haired, and skinny. At four and a half, reserved and responsible, he had to take care of the other two. He didn't have time for foolishness. Sissy, only a seven-month bambino.

I'm sure the people who saw us could not imagine what an American family with such little kids were doing wondering the streets of Athens. In spite of the mixed-up hours and problems with sleeping, we had an enjoyable time in Athens. It was a great place to help make the time transition.

Our scheduled time to leave Athens airport was 7:00 that evening. When we got there, we were told our plane had not even left Germany yet. The airline put us up in a small modern hotel near the airport. Since we were to eat on the plane, the airlines also bought our supper. We were able to eat in a fashion more like we were accustomed to. We rested, waited for time to pass, and went back to the airport at about 2:00 a.m.. Once again, the handsome young man in the customs area was back at work. He and Monte took up where they had left off a few nights before. We said our goodbyes and were on our way to Addis Ababa on Ethiopian Airlines with a stop in Cairo and Asmara.

Ethiopian Airlines looked much different than the previous planes. The Ethiopian plane had lots of green, and the Lion of Judah symbol. Boarding that flight, it felt like we were going into another world. We were leaving the countries of the western dress and moving into a culture with flowing white clothing, and significantly stranger language. The smells also changed as the incense and spices came strong. We landed in Cairo at about sunup. Then flew over the huge, barren Sahara Desert, and desolate country. The flight followed the Nile, a great winding ribbon going through all that desert land, and then, landed in Asmara.

We were in Ethiopia where the American government had an airbase with a sizeable American community. We flew on, following the Nile, and the terrain changing dramatically. From above, we could see areas of extremely deep chasms, high plains with sharp, deep drop-offs. It took us an hour to make that flight. Later we learned that if you were to drive that road, it would take several days. The road between Asmara and Addis was extremely hazardous, not only because of the terrain and poor road conditions, but also because of the "shiftas" who were always waiting for the opportunity to rob any, and all vehicles that came along.

A beautiful sunny day, January 16, 1961, when we stepped off that plane in Addis Ababa. We were met by an Ethiopian representative who took us through customs, easily and quickly. Relieved, as I had a pistol in the bottom of my purse. I didn't appreciate being a "pistol packin' mama," but Zeke thought it was necessary to have it.

Six weeks prior to our arrival in Ethiopia they had experienced a coup d'état and there had been lots of fighting, and much destruction. As a result, they had banned guns being brought into the country. Zeke had planned to take his rifles and shotgun along. He intended to hunt, but had to leave them in Oklahoma. He wasn't happy about the new regulation. That was one of the main reasons for his wanting to go to Africa. A bit of explanation: in those days, one was disturbed about going through customs' many rules as to what could be brought into a country, or taken out.

We were met by the entire Oklahoma group stationed in Addis. The head of the party was Bonnie Nicholson, with his wife, Leah. Hugh and Hazel Rouk were our chief greeters. Hugh would be Zeke's boss. They put us up in their home for a few days, did not want to send us to the hotel since the kids were so young, and eating in a hotel would surely bring us immediate problems. Food was a concern.

Other members of the Oklahoma group were all extension workers and served in much the same capacity as our county agents did in the States. The Arnolds were a middle-aged couple. They had grown children. He, Dan, was head of that group. He had served as county agent in Woods County some years before and knew Dad. All the extension people lived in the same compound. That included the Beards, Warkentines and the Montgomerys. Bob Lee was the writer, photographer, and public relation man for the Oklahoma Contract.

The airport was a short distance from the compound which the Rouks and Nicholsons shared. Interesting how we were immediately introduced to the driving conditions, and overall picture of Addis and Ethiopia. We traveled on one of the most driven streets in Addis. We had just gotten off a modern jet, landing at a modern airport, and moved into a different time zone. The road scenes introduced us to a strange world.

Driving in Hazel's American car, we saw little run down dukas (shops) beside a modern looking store front. Fiats, Volkswagens, Mercedes, lorries (trucks), and buses. Natives and donkeys shared the tarmac road. Side streets were dirt paths and some wide enough for Land Rovers. Donkeys loaded with all types of wares, followed by a shabbily dressed man with a toga like wrap on his head. Ladies laden with giant sized water pots carried on their heads. Filthy beggars, dirty fly-covered kids contrasted the elegant native dressed in a white shama with colorful border. It is impossible to put into words, the changes felt when appearing in such a strange environment, knowing that those conditions would be our home for at least two years. We had anticipated these moments for the last couple of months and now it was reality.

The compound, where the Rouks lived, had two houses, made from native rock. The houses were special because they had indoor kitchens. Many of the houses had outdoor kitchens. Most living rooms and dining areas were quite spacious as people entertained a lot. Houses were generally two or three bedrooms and seldom more than one bathroom. Floors were hard, marble type tiles, and most window sills made of marble. There were no closets, or built-ins, in any of the houses. Everything reflected European style.

Since the Rouks had only two bedrooms, we arranged makeshift beds for the kids. Steve slept on a fold-out lawn chair in the hall and the other two kids slept in the room with us. They still had their days and nights all mixed up and didn't go to sleep till the wee hours of the morning. It really bothered me to think that they were keeping the Rouks awake at night. Hazel was gracious and insisted it was no big imposition. Hugh had his toddies before bedtime and the kids wouldn't bother his sleep. Hazel had a cook who did all the baking and cooking. While we were there, we only had food that came out of a box or a tin. Hazel did not want the kids to adjust to too many things at once. She knew the local food: meats, fruits and veggies would present a problem for them. The first day, we rested, tried to adjust, and unwind. I felt like I was floating for several days after I came down out of the clouds and wondered if the kids felt the same. It was good for us to just go outside and sit in the warm beautiful sunshine and watch the strange sights through the compound gate. The walls were like six-foot tall, the iron gate always locked. The guard or gardener unlocked the gate when he was summoned by the honking of an arriving car. Being on the main road going into Addis, people and donkeys were constantly passing. There were lots of peddlers and beggars coming to the gate. It seemed like constant noise and confusion. The kids and I enjoyed the unusual sights. The second day, the kids stayed with Hazel and the houseboy while Mrs. Nicholson took me to the Embassy and introduced me to the Ambassador's wife. I felt like I was really somebody special since it was just the three of us having coffee. It was nice to know that they cared enough to want to know the Americans coming into the area.

Wednesday, we moved into a temporary house. Hazel took me to the commissary where we got a supply of canned and boxed goods. Driving in Hazel's big American car, we were immediately flanked by natives when we stopped in front of the commissary. Wealthy Americans driving big cars were coming and going all day long. It was the perfect place for beggars to congregate and the place to be if you were looking for a job. Could I ever adjust to the sight of beggars? I had seen them and heard them at the compound gate, but nothing in comparison to this. Filthy, dressed in rags, carrying walking sticks; some blind, some maimed, some with leprosy, or elephantiasis, always a depressing sight. That was when you realize how fortunate you are. At first, you wanted to help them all. Oh. the shocking sights! After a while, you come to the realization that beggars were everyplace and was the best profession in Africa. Often children were maimed at birth so they could be assured of a good living. Winding our way through the beggars, a mamita (house girl) came to us carrying a letter. She was looking for work for 50.00 Ethie ($20.00 American) a month. Hazel thought her letter was legitimate. She was clean, and suggested I hire her. Hazel knew I would need help immediately. We would not have a washing machine until the sea freight came.

Shocked at seeing the commissary being so small, a rock building and no windows. One entrance made it difficult for thieves. No children allowed inside due to crowded conditions, rat poison scattered about. They had a wider variety than I expected, no brand choices, but all the necessities. Some tinned items came from Europe, especially meats and cheese. Liquor so cheap that you couldn't afford not to drink. Drambouie cost $3.00 a bottle. Cigarettes $2.20 a carton. Food priced about the same as in Montana. In the commissary, we paid everything with an American check. Mamete waited outside so she could ride with us to the house. Practically impossible to give instructions on how to find a place—there were no street names, it was either "show me" or draw a picture.

Wonderful to be in a house, although they did not want us to have that arrangement permanent. Too far from other Americans and not in a good area. We would either move to Bishoftu or find us a house in or near another American compound.

We had left Montana the 22nd of December and moved into a house in Ethiopia, January 13. An overwhelming relief to do without considering someone else first. The kids could play outside within the rock compound wall, a big iron gate, and kept a guard, Begge. He was larger than most Ethiopians and belonged to the Galla tribe. He lived in the servant quarters and "guarded" the house day and night. The yard's bare ground had no trees or grass. The guards usually had handmade bamboo whistles used to whistle at one another during the night. I think that was just to keep them from sleeping too soundly. Asfo, whom we always called Mamete (servant girl who cares for children) came to work at 7:00 a.m. I had quite a time telling her what time to come. She spoke no English and I had learned no Amheric. That was our first obstacle with language barrier. I was aware of the difference in our clocks. Their days started at 6:00 a.m. so 7:00 a.m. was one o'clock and then you just counted around the clock. There was no AM or PM. Mamete was an enthusiastic worker and eager to please. We got along exceptionally well. She was happy with her wages of $50.00 Ehie, or $20.00 American. A very good wage and Hazel suggested that I not give her any raise as that was already a lot.

We settled into the house quickly. Mamete got right with the cleaning and the place was already in GOOD shape. Furniture already in the house, we only had to unpack our suitcases. Our air freight had not arrived. There was a survival kit that had most necessities. We borrowed the rest.

The kids loved it! They were home! The boys played outside. It was beautiful during the day. The Lee's loaned us a play pen for Sissy so she could be on the veranda. The house, a three-bedroom rock structure, had a big veranda in front. Quickly, Mamete and I got into a routine. We didn't have a washing machine. She did all the washing in the bath tub, daily, in the mornings, hung the clothes outside to dry, and ironed them in the afternoon. All clothes had to be ironed due to an insect which often got onto the clothes, and if it got onto the body would burrow under the skin and cause sores.

The heat from the iron killed the little varmints. While Memeta ironed, we had Amheric lessons. I had realized I had to learn the language, at least enough so she and I could converse. We started by pointing out items. I learned nouns, and after a while, we began to add verbs. I got a book to help. Amheric was the chief language of Ethiopia; however, due to many tribes, there were also many other languages. Even though one knew Amheric, it would not always get you by while traveling the country. After several weeks, Memeta and I could carry on a pretty good conversation that at least the two of us knew what we were talking about. I still found it difficult talking to someone else. Memeta understood my strange pronunciation and she used the words that I knew. We sort of had our own language.

We had been living off the commissary food for several weeks, then we were invited to the Beards for dinner. I was amazed. They ate lettuce, tomatoes, and fresh fruits. Wow! We had some dinner. And we ate them! I knew we would eat cooked vegetables, but I didn't realize anyone ate fresh raw ones. Well, if they ate them, and were still among the living, I decided to try it. The next time I went to the vegetable market, I bought some. We washed all vegetables and fruits well. We started by soaking them in bleach water for fifteen or twenty minutes, then rinse them several times in water and finished by rinsing in boiled water. Anything that could be peeled was safe to eat and cooking was best. "Addisites" was very common and you were always fortunate if you only had a case of the "trots." Amoebic dysentery was common. The first time I went to the market, I bought tangerines. They were wonderful. Since we hadn't had any fresh fruit in a long time, we all ate too many. I went to the farm and called Hazel to see what I should do about Sissy. She had a bad case of diarrhea. Hazel came by and took us to the doctor. We were told that she only had a case of "too many tangerines."

The Beards invited us to a non-denomination church service on a Sunday morning. We also attended Lutheran services in the afternoon. We met the Wrights who lived in Bishoftu and the Hallidays from Stockton, California. Wayne Halliday was with the Water Resource group, also associated with the Point Four Program. Lydia Halliday was amazed to hear that I had not been to the meat market. She said she would be over on Monday to take me to the shop. That was a real experience! Upon entering, we had to flip aside the long colorful plastic strips hanging in the doorway. Those were the fly chasers and were to keep the flies out. It seemed they also kept them in and I really don't know how they could have gotten more flies in there.

Chunks of meat scattered about. You needed to order what you wanted. Lydia asked me, "What do you want?" How did I know? I told her to go ahead and get what she wanted. I was still in a state of shock. I just said, "I will take the same as you are getting," which was ground meat, ground twice through a course grinder. That way if you caught a fly in the operation, you wouldn't be able to identify it. We also got a chunk or two of meat for roast. Everything weighed in kilos and the butcher didn't understand English. We thoroughly washed all meats before cooking; however, it wasn't possible to wash the "mincemeat." Burger was called mincemeat. We also went to the vegetable market and felt a lot more comfortable than the first time.

I nearly got into trouble when we came back to the states after years of calling it "mincemeat." When I ordered a half of beef and giving the cutting orders, I asked for the rest to be "mincemeat." I really had them confused. Later, I realized what I had done and explained I did not want American mincemeat.

It was quite a change to find different foods, a new unit of measure, different money, and a strange language.

Hugh and Hazel Rouk came by and took us to Bishoftu to see the town and the experiment farm, and check on housing. We had decided we would move to Bishoftu if we could find a suitable house. Zeke was spending a lot of time on the road and Steve was not old enough to go to school, so we wouldn't have a problem that way for a year. Zeke would be home for lunch. The kids and I were excited about the trip and anxious to get settled in someplace.

Bishoftu was about one hour down country from Addis, southeast. On our way out of Addis, on the main "highway," we approached a stop light, which was rather an unusual sight as they used traffic circles. The road became a one-way, under the railroad track, and the light controlled the one-way traffic. The light was red and a taxi driver stopped in front of us. It seemed he needed to relieve himself. Since they didn't know about bathrooms, he just got out and took care of his business. When the light turned green, he had not finished, he waved us on.

The road we traveled on was tarmac, two lanes, but side roads were narrow dirt roads, mostly paths for people and donkeys. Addis was at an altitude of seven-thousand to ten-thousand feet, and drops as you move toward Bishoftu making it a much warmer climate and lacking vegetation. Basically, that was farming country, grain crops. They had just finished the harvesting and preparing for the rainy season, and next seasons' crops.

A fascinating trip where I always enjoyed the primitive sights, enhanced by the exotic odors, and the captivating, haunting music coming from the dukas (stores) as we traveled through the villages. I used to think a lot about Marge Fehrer and Alice Bandy, favorite friends, and wished they could have ridden with me just one time to experience the strange world. They would have loved it as much as I did.

Native cooking was done outside. Much of the wood used was eucalyptus which gives off a wonderful odor, coupled with the smell of spices used to prepare the wat (stew). The music along the main street of the two villages was always very loud.

Driving into Bishoftu, (meaning stinking fish) now changed to Debra Zeit (hill of olives) we passed the Lutheran Mission High School, sitting on a small hill. We left the main highway and followed main street with dukas on either side of the street. We heard traditional music and smelled the same odors as other villages. Except for the occasional hill, the terrain was flat, and then the road widened to a wide powdery dust, the open market to the right. That wasn't a market day, road not heavily traveled. Market day was twice a week, and on those days, people and donkeys carrying wares to and from the market place. Continuing, we came to the experiment station, the airbase at the end of the road.

The farm consisted of several tin buildings with tin roofs. Zeke's crude office occupied a corner of one of the tin buildings with plenty of bird exposure. There were plans for expansion in the near future, as soon as the funds became available. Billy Webb had left Debra Zeit. Zeke replaced him. They had a good start on the planting and growing of crops, testing the experimental program.

At the station, we met the thirteen educated men who oversaw the projects. Most of them had been educated at the Jimma high school and college in Alameya. Several had been to the states to further their education. They were friendly and a pleasure to meet, and seemed happy to have us there. After touring the farm, we went back to the hotel to view the crater lake which it overlooked, had lunch, and introduced to the Italian way of eating. Italians ran most of the restaurants. Pasta always served before the main course, mainly spaghetti, and some had lasagna. We were told filet mignon steak was the best thing to order. It would always be freshly cooked and hot, and served with fresh vegetables. That was the safest thing to eat. We did not eat the salad. The filet was the only cut of meat tender enough and that's what we bought at the meat market. Since water was unsafe, we had Ambo water, which was a safe mineral water, or Sinalco a brand of pop available, bottled by the Italians.

Since we were probably moving to Bishoftu, we looked at a large house that was available for rent. It had mud walls, few windows, and no indoor kitchen. Then we drove through the area, near the lake's edge to check more housing, mostly owned by government officials who kept a vacation home, but lived in Addis. They came to Bishoftu during the rainy season where it was warmer and drier. The houses covered about one fourth of the lake's edge. The remainder of the lake was void of people living near it. The Swedish working at the airbase occupied most of the other housing in the area, away from the lake. Much of the residences were made of brick with traditional tin roof.

Zeke and Hugh were in favor of our moving to Bishoftu. Hazel and Lela Nicholson warned against moving. They said once we settled there, they would never permit us to move to Addis, and concerned I would get lonely. We would be isolated from the American community. The Wrights, from the mission, were the only Americans in the Bishoftu area.

Zeke felt he would be on the road a lot and would spend more time at home if he did not need to drive to Bishoftu to work, especially with traveling being dangerous. I later found out that Hazel and Leah knew what they were talking about, but too late.

We went to Bishoftu one day just to look at available houses. It was disappointing. There were only several to see and were located right along with the native houses, all constructed the same—walls made from chika, dirt, and straw. We were looking at "big" houses with windows and it had to have an indoor kitchen. Several were available with windows, but they were still dark and had musty odor, hallways very narrow, "depressing." So that is just how it is when you have dirt floors.

Tesfye, Zeke's African counterpart, took us out and he thought of another house. It belonged to Digesmach Mangasha Sium who would be moving to the Tigre province, far north Ethiopia. His position would be much like our governor. His wife was Princess Aida who was the granddaughter of Emperor, Haile Salassie. They had a weekend home on the lake's edge, about a mile from the hotel, and half mile from the farm. He thought they would be willing to rent it. We waited for him to contact them. We looked at the house a few days later. They were interested renting it to us as this would bring them a much higher rent from an American. It was a two-bedroom red brick with a large living room and dining room. It had an indoor kitchen with a tiny, tiny sink in the corner. That was the only way you could tell it was intended to be a kitchen. All floors were a marble type tile. There were shutters on the windows. When closed, covered the whole window, latched inside. They had added the shutters for security purposes. The kids would share the largest bedroom—roomy enough for three beds and a bit, and a large, wide, spacious hall, large enough for two big wardrobes. No built-ins of any kind in any of the houses. Oklahoma Contract supplied all European type furnishings. The bathroom was large and contained a most fascinating piece of equipment, a bidet and the kids were always intrigued by it. They thought it great as a a foot washer. The front of the house faced the crater lake, about a half kilometer downhill. Beautiful sight out of the dining room and living room windows. The wall was mostly glass doors. We had a nice front yard, grass and a grape arbor. The house was like a mansion compared to the others. If the construction had been better, it would have cost considerable in the states. It also had what they considered a guest house, a small room off the outside back entrance. It had a half bath.

We moved in immediately.

Oklahoma Contract provided the furniture. We had received our air freight. It didn't take long to settle in. We only had had clothes and bare necessities. We anxiously awaited for our sea freight. Especially the kids needed things for entertainment. The weather was great so they could be outside much of the time. The cool rainy season was coming. We had a fireplace. We had used the one in Addis as the only means for heating. It was chilly. An air conditioner would have been more useful in Debra Zeit, but that was unheard of.

The week after we moved into the house, Zeke had to leave for a full week on a trip to the college in Alameya. They wanted him to get some insight as to what was happening, meet other staff members, and get familiar with the program. He flew to Dire Dawa, in the Harar Province. The kids and I were in the house for a full week without any real contact with the outside world, except for the guys from the farm occasionally coming over to check on us. We had no transportation, no telephone, no friends, and of course no radio, TV or newspaper. I was frightened and slept with a gun under my pillow. The pistol I had smuggled in at the airport. I knew how to load it and shoot it. I would probably have been in more trouble if I had tried to use it. Tesfye felt we would have no trouble with thieves anyway as the house belonged to the royal family. It was not wise to steal from royalty, penalties were severe if you did.

We had brought along the same gardener and house girl we had while in Addis. They both lived in the servant quarters. We also had to hired a night guard. We had a giant-sized yard and we didn't have a wall around the compound.

That week passed slow for the kids and me, but Tesfye and Haile Mariam came over several times to check on us. The kids and I didn't have much for entertainment but I had a piece of fabric. I made Lynette a dress, all by hand, with lots of tucks and lace to make it last a while. I learned lots of Amheric.

We had some distinguished guests. The kids and I were outside when this elegantly dressed middle-aged man came riding up on a great white horse, waving its fly-swisher tail. He was a sign of wealth. That fascinating guest intrigued us. I had mixed feelings as one had to be so careful whom we could trust. He spoke good British English. Told us he was Digesmach Basaab who lived two houses over from us and used the house as a vacation home. He had come over to meet and welcome us to his country. He told the kids about his pet monkey. Later, the monkey did come for a visit. It could come right in through the open windows, found the bananas real quick, and good at hiding under the bed.

Then Sunday we had another surprise. I had just washed by hair, had it up in rollers, and wearing an old housecoat when an Army jeep came into the drive, followed by another and another and another. I think six, with armed officers appearing all over the place and then I saw a familiar face. By that time Mamete was in the house with me and being very protective. Tesfy, from the farm, and Bege, the gardener, were bringing the dignified gentleman to meet me and this was Digesmach Mangasha Sium. He had come to see if we wanted anything before they moved to Tigre province. The Digesmach was returning from a week at the lakes and would be moving soon. Embarrassed about my appearance, what could I say? He did not want to come in the house but wanted to walk the garden and visit. His wife was not with him. She had already gone on to Addis with the children. We walked and talked about the garden and the banana trees, and went around to the front of the house at the swimming pool. It was about 10'x24', and 4' deep. It looked terrific, oval shaped, made from concrete and a tile bottom. One problem, the tile bottom leaked like a sieve, impossible to keep water. We would have a water shortage later. I would've preferred to fill it up with dirt. We talked about the pool. I worried about it since the kids were small. It was dangerous with or without water. I told him I'd like some paint for the inside of the house. He said he would send someone over immediately to do it. I didn't want that to happen. I had seen their painting and the type of brushes they used. I didn't think that would be much of an improvement. They used a kind of a white wash and the brush was like broom straw tied together. I mean crude, they'd slopped it all around a bit, and there would be as much on the floor as anyplace else. They were accustomed to painting houses made of mud. I told him I would like to buy some imported paint and I would do the work myself. This was unheard of to him.

If that was what I wanted, he would buy the paint. He had not heard of an American woman doing that kind of work. He stayed for about half an hour. We had had a nice visit, and he said his wife would come to visit sometime when they came back to Addis. The convoy of military jeeps left as quickly as they had arrived and the kids and I had had another interesting experience.

When Zeke returned from Alameya, he filled us in on the happenings around there. Since it was a larger American community, I was eagerly awaiting the time when we could make a trip to the college.

Life got boring quickly. Nothing to do, no place to go, and the kids and I home alone. We read stories, played outside, and had lots of tea parties. I asked Zeke to get me the paint in Addis. That would give me something to do. He was always "too busy to get it." Good paint was not available in Bishoftu.

In Addis we went shopping for a car and decided on an Opel station wagon, a special order from Germany. We also had considered a Volkswagen, or a Peugot. That would've required a waiting period of a month, or two. We would get it into the country without paying customs. Foreign cars looked so small when we looked at them in the states, but now that we were over in Africa they looked normal and the American cars looked so large.

Often, when things happened, they all happened at once. I finally got Zeke to get me some paint. I started to work. Within a week we heard that the sea freight was in Jabute, African port, would soon arrive in Addis, and would need to get it through customs. That was April. Getting the sea freight was exciting. We had lots of new things, and even if it was old, it was so long since we had packed it, it was like new. In addition to the basic, there would be clothes, pots and pans, dishes, toys, and books,

I got my sewing machine, washing machine, and freezer. The servants were shocked when they saw all the things we had. They had never worked for Americans before. When Mamete saw the sewing machine, she told me she would do all the work, and wanted me to sew some clothes for her and her daughter. We had quite an experience teaching her how to use the washing machine and wringer. She never did get the hang of the wringer. She would always put too much in it. We had diapers and they went around the wringer too easy. Anyway, she never mastered it and after I had to cut one of my good blouses out of the wringer we compromised, took the wringer off the machine. She didn't use it anymore, or I did the washing myself.

Then the Opel arrived, I was so mad at Zeke that it would probably have caused a divorce right then but what could I do in Africa? For weeks, the kids and I had talked about the day when the car would arrive. Zeke would take us to town and drive home together in our new car. We were suffering from cabin fever. The kids had not been anyplace, except for church on Sunday, in weeks. I had only been to Addis five or six times. Anyway, it was time for Zeke to be home from work. Then we heard a horn and ran to the door. We were not expecting anyone and there he was! Driving the new car. We had not gone to Addis to bring it home. I was furious, so he was too. He said, "You would have been happier if I had brought a loaf of bread," to which I had to agree. After all, we hadn't had a loaf of bread other than homemade since we arrived.

The guys at the farm were wonderful to me. Tesfye was the assistant or counterpart to Zeke. He was the one who had connection with the Digesmach, whose house we rented. Tesfye had connections with the Emperor. Haile Mariam Lemma was the character of the bunch. He had a big mouth and he really used it for laughing. He had been educated in the states and when Zeke was gone he would come over often and vowed he liked the company, but I knew he just came to share my Salem cigarettes. Since he had spent time in the states, he knew the life of the American woman and knew how different being in Ethiopia was for me. He also enjoyed playing with the kids. They loved to have him come. Then there was Wodena, the handsome one who was tall, slim, well-built, and had a sweet smile and twinkle in his eyes. You might say I fell in love with him. He was as quiet as Haile Mariam was talkative. Only one of the guys was married, Seifoo, who was very short and chunky. He had two young sons and talked about his kids a lot. I saw the boys a few times, but never met his wife. Wives were never brought out. Their place in life was to stay home, take care of the household.

Thirteen guys in all on the staff heading up the different departments from horticulture to agronomy, to chickens and cattle. All had been educated in Jimma and Alameya and only a few had been to the states. I didn't get to know any of the others well. They were younger and not as well educated.

The farm had been set up by Oklahoma State University to assist the farmers in the area in developing new and better methods of farming, geared to their type of living. Their methods were very, very primitive, much like Bible days. Ethiopia was the only African country which used a plough, and oxen used to pull it. That was the simple type, much like our push cultivators, with a single blade, pulled by the ox, followed by a native keeping the plough in the hard-dry ground.

Planting crops was done by hand and broadcasting method used for sowing grain crops. While Zeke was there, they did introduce the hand cultivator. That worked well for the trial plots on the grains and horticulture crops. Since that was brought in from the states, farmers did not have access to those at that time. Crops were harvested with a scythe. They trod the grain from straw with oxen, like Bible times.

The farm had been set up to help teach the farmers how they might improve methods and help produce new and better varieties of crops—grains, grasses, legumes, and horticulture crops, make them heartier, more disease resistant, and improve conditions in general. The growing season was rather short. Other seasons were rainy or dry. Many variety of diseases were not hardy enough to bear up under the conditions.

The U.S. Government came through with a large sum of money. Although it took a great deal of time to get things started, Zeke had the opportunity to accomplish a lot.

They built a small office building from cement blocks. Zeke and Tesfye had offices in a building with windows and a ceiling, and could even lock the door. They hired an Ethiopian girl as secretary.

With the additional funds, they introduced the American chicken to Ethiopia. Eggs and incubators came from the states. It was an exciting day when those little chickens started to pop out of the eggs. Many of the natives knew nothing about that strange method of producing baby chickens. All went well until the chickens got sick. Zeke contacted the veterinarian from the college and he came to diagnose. They had the chicken pox and all would need to be vaccinated. It took all weekend to accomplish the job. The chickens survived and went on to being yummy American fried chicken in a few months. The natives didn't like our chickens. The meat was "too soft." Their chickens had to scratch for a survival. They were small and produced tough, stringy, dark meat and were not susceptible to chicken pox. The American community in Addis loved the chickens. If you wanted to get Zeke upset, remind him that the Embassy referred to Bishoftu as the "chicken farm" and there would be trouble. Those fat, tender chickens were popular with all the Americans. We had visitors from Jimma and Alamaya who came to share our good fortune. One family came and stayed with us for two days so they could butcher, package, and freeze them to take back to Jimma.

Another addition was the improved beef product. Like the chickens, the local beef was very tough, skinny, horns wider than the animal, and heavy for the skinny animal to carry. The cattle had little grass to graze on and most of the time it was miles to get to water. They were never able to fatten, and unheard of to feed them. The animal had to walk to market. By the time they got there, they had lost more weight. Imported cattle could not survive, susceptible to disease, and conditions. Ticks were extremely bad. The animals had to be walked through dips quite often. Without the dip, an animal crossed between local and foreign would never survive. They did some cross breeding and produced better breeds. They did some testing on those animals by feeding them processed food, and found they produced superior beef.

A substantial amount of money became available for beautification, testing flowers, shrubs, bougainvillea, lantana, hibiscus, etc. We were there long enough to witness the beauty. They did extremely well during the rainy season. I enjoyed going over to the farm and bring home an armload of tea roses, all colors, many varieties. I could keep an arrangement of several dozen roses on my brass table from India, and they were so beautiful. Many changes took place at the farm during the two years while there. The natives expressed satisfaction with Zeke and the results.

The Emperor had a palace along the edge of the same crater lake we lived on. He often came to Debra Zeit. He wanted the surrounding to remain quiet so no motor boats were allowed. The lake was a beautiful sight when seeing the occasional sail boat. Located on the lip of the crater, we could see down onto the water. Sometimes, when the Emperor came to Debra Zeit, he would go over to the farm and check on progress. Tesfye would show him around.

One Sunday afternoon, Zeke went over to the farm for a few minutes and returned a few hours later. He was quite excited. The Emperor, Haile Selassie had been there. Since Tesfye was not available, Zeke showed the Emperor around. They had walked and talked for about an hour. Zeke didn't have that opportunity again. I didn't have a chance to meet the Emperor. We met his motor caravan a few times. When meeting the Emperor's caravan, natives stopped, bowed low to the ground while he passed. We would stop the car, get out, and stand at attention.

Near the Emperor's palace there was a hotel. Occasionally the boys from the farm and I would go to there for dinner. They always invited me when they had something special. I felt comfortable being a part of it. They were pleased when I joined. They told me, Mrs. Webb, wife of the former American there would never join them. I told the guys I would have them over for an American dinner. They couldn't wait. The first time I entertained them, they ate every bite I had prepared and it disappeared fast. I wanted to fix food that I felt they would like, so we had beef, vegetables, salad, homemade French bread, and pie. I had expected them to take several pieces of bread. The first time around, they each took like a half a loaf. I was shocked. I had baked a few loaves. I had enough. The dinner was a huge success. They gladly came back for American food anytime I invited them. One time they came over and had a local drum or two. They proceeded to beat out a chant, then the guys did a native dance around the living room. Now I wish I would have made a video tape, but who ever heard of such a thing.

Now that I had the Opel, I would go to Addis anytime. After several months of hibernation, I was anxious to go. I had not realized how long it would take to get the car, the freight and opportunity for friends and a bit of a social life. At first, I went into Addis nearly every week to attend ladies Point 4 meetings, sewing groups, coffee parties, etc., Most of the time the kids stayed home with the Mamete. After a bit of that, I decided that it was just taking too much of a chance. One time I came home and all my jewelry was scattered on the front porch and the kids were having a wonderful time with it. I told Mamete to let the work go and just spend time with the kids. That made no difference. She didn't know what was acceptable behavior and what was not. Her daughter, Sode, who was about ten, came to the house, also. When in the house, the kids would have a really great time in the living room.

By that time, Sissy could barely walk. She had climbed up on top of the teacart, which had wheels and was standing on it in front of the big living room window. Scared me to death before I could get her down. I was afraid if I excited her, we really would have a problem. I decided to use servants for babysitting only when necessary, just too frightening to trust them alone.

Driving in Ethiopia was challenging. The first time I went into Addis, I left the kids home with the Mamete and took the gardener along. I felt more comfortable than going alone. He was more than happy to go with me. That made him look like a big shot. Besides that, it got him out of working. We had just left the housing area and were on the very wide, dusty market road, which would take us past the native market and through Debra Zeit, when one of the native woman came running across the road. I saw her headed toward me. I slammed on the brakes. She ran right into the side of my stopped car. She had feared getting hit by an Army jeep that was coming toward her from the other direction and knew that if she was in its way, it would hit her. In those parts, it was start your engine, start your horn, blare on through, if you hit someone, kill them so you didn't have to go through a hassle, There were big problems if you just injured someone. Burial was cheap. They would not only want hospital but also disability. and If you killed someone, it was the cost of a box. Fortunate I was never involved in an accident, although we had a few close encounters.

An American from Addis hit a girl just outside of Debra Zeit. He came to the house to get help. Zeke was away in Addis. What could I say? We put the girl in the back of my Opel station wagon and I took her to the hospital in Bishoftu. I'd told Mamete in my best Amheric, but didn't take the time to write Zeke a note. I had anticipated being back in two hours, maximum, against my better judgement. I waited with the uncle as they treated the little girl since they needed a ride back home. She had a broken leg so they kept her and we didn't get back home till dark. The American wanted me to bring the little girl's relative to Addis when I went back. I waited for the outcome of the injury. By the time I got back to Bishoftu it was already dark. Zeke had been pacing the floor, he couldn't get any answers from anyone. The kids had told him I had gone with some police so that didn't make it any better. Mamete was no help with her story. He visualized all sorts of things and was really upset with me for not leaving a note. It was not very smart on my part. Told him that maybe he got a bit of understanding as I was the one at home, not know what was going on, and we didn't have much connection with the outside world. Later, I was really put out with that American. I went to the farm and called him at home to get my blanket back, the one we had used for the girl. I called him at home and left a message with his wife. Would you believe he called the station and told them I shouldn't call his house again. He did not want his wife to be upset or disturbed by the matter. He had two more accidents during his two-year period over there. He was lucky he didn't end up in jail. They did get him out of the country quickly after the third accident. It cost a lot to get an American out of jail and it certainly was not a pleasant place to be. If there was no family to look after prisoners, they would sit there and die without food or drink.

Coming from Oklahoma and Montana, the Ethiopian food was a drastic change. I grew up on pork, potatoes, and gravy, lots of onions, and green beans. Knew nothing about spicy foods. Was introduced to tacos in Montana. They were done with tomato soup, no spice. I had already discovered how different coffee could be when we got to Europe. That Greek coffee was strong. They mixed it with hot milk, pouring both together. Ethiopian boona was served in little cups and heavy with sugar. I came to like it as a special treat. They drank a honey wine called Tej and it was served in a special bottle. Talla was their beer made from wheat, barley, or corn. The basic bread was injera which was a thin bread made from teff and water and the mixture sat for a few days as it became a bubbly sour dough. Then cooked over an open fire, poured from a tin can round and round till it reached the center that took about five minutes. The injera became their tablecloth, napkin, and bread as it was stacked on the injera basket in layers. Tear off a piece, sop it in the wat, fold it over and yum. The favorite wat was doro, or chicken, which was spicy, and always served with a boiled egg. Berbere was the blend of spices most used, heavy on the red peppers. First time Mamete made some for us, she brought the spice in half-full baby food jar, and put it in our *doro* wat. Later, I said *bazoo mook* (very hot) and her reply was *tinish mook*, Madame (tiny hot). We really came to like the food but required learning to like hot and spicy. Since Orthodox Christians fast many days in the year, they ate lentil and vegetable wat most of the time. Many got sick after holidays and end of fasting. They couldn't tolerate eating that much meat. The men had a festive way to eat meat while celebrating. Cut off a good-sized chunk, raw of course, sunk in teeth, and took a good big bite, getting out the sharp knife, and cutting off that bite from the chunk with an upward slice. Pass it on to the next person. Not much fun to watch. They also liked the ground meat loaded with berbere and that was eaten raw, too.

We were invited to Jima, location of the high school where Americans with our group were on the staff. Several of the families had lunch with us and some had even come to dress out chickens at our house to take back and put in their freezers. Mamete was super at that and even seemed to enjoy doing it. We always worked with her. Since we only had two bedrooms, families stayed in Addis. We drove to Jima in a Land Rover and spent several nights. We also had time to enjoy the culture around there. That was an area with more rainfall, more green, growing plants, and different style housing Roofs were much more peaked and needed more than adobe type construction.

Great for the kids and me to be away for a few days and experience a change. We bought some baskets. A popular thing in Ethiopia. The colors were great. They used a lot of bright pink, purple and turquoise in that part of the country. On our return home, we were so thankful that they sent us away with plenty of water and snacks. The Land Rover just quit about an hour out of Jima. Water pump broke. We needed a replacement. Nothing to do but sit and wait till someone came by and stopped to help. We were in luck. One of the Americans from the school came by after an hour or so of waiting. He could get the water pump in Jima, bring it to us, and help in the replacement. Many curious people came by while waiting. They would get bored after a while and leave. The trip was about 5 hours. Delayed, but all was well.

Later we went to the college at Alameya. We had to go by plane. More to see and do there. We did go to Basket Mary's shop where the ladies all sat around in an upstairs room, weaving baskets. That was a special place, even written up in Reader's Digest about that time. Specialty was the injera basket, used as a table, large round, and always had a dome lid. Different colors, mostly red and blue. Dyes came from local plants, etc.. I tried basket weaving once and found out what an art that it is, and takes much practice. Weaving material must be soft and pliable.

We went to see the Hyena Man. No one went to Harar without watching that sight. There were many of these dirty, nasty, noisy at night, and ugly animals throughout the country. At night, they were always searching for food. Legend has it that the "hyena man" started calling in the animals years ago as a way of protecting people and animals. Fed them so they wouldn't be out destroying property. We parked outside of Harar, headlights beaming in the direction of the feed. Then the noise began, clattering of bones along with the chattering of the man. It made a really eerie sight and sound. The hyenas came right up to the man and fed them from his hand. WOW!

Nice to be around other American families. They all lived on the campus and families had a lot of togetherness. Yep, I was a bit jealous. We were going back to being "home alone." Back to my

28

teaching Steve to read etc. using Calvert's correspondence course. The other two had Sode, Mamete's daughter for a playmate, while Steve and I had school each morning.

One fine day I had some most unexpected visitors. Once again, Tesfye came along with cars and guards. He came to introduce me to Princess Aida who was the owner of the house. Princess Tenagnework, her mother, known for her work with children, and her younger sister, Sophia were also with her. "So now what do I do?" The mother did not say much but the two sisters were easy to talk with. We really had a nice visit. I made a huge mistake when I had Mamete bring us ice tea. The mother was not in to ice so she asked for hot tea. I should have known better. I had been working on my braided rug and they were intrigued by that. Both sisters got down on the floor and crawled around on the rug to see how it was done. I had collected used wool garments, which I had washed and stripped while in the states. By that time, it was about 6x8 feet and of many colors. Our visit was so great that they invited me to the palace. "Now why didn't I have enough smarts to set a date?" I never did and that has been one of the greatest regrets in my lifetime. I could have gone to the palace of Haile Selassie!

During World War II, the Italians took over the country. At the end of the war, Emperor, Haile Selassie returned to reign Ethiopia. He allowed missions and others to come and help develop the country. That brought the Point 4 program and the Lutheran mission. In 1959. the Mekane Yesus mission started. When we arrived in 1961, it was growing and made up of about eight or more families—a builder, a doctor, two nurses, a few preachers, and a teacher. They also had a radio station that aired into the country. Sunday mornings, were reserved for services in Amharic. They had a number of Ethiopians involved with the mission. We attended the Sunday afternoon English services in Addis, along with the mission people and others. Wonderful to have a great connection, and Bob, a single preacher, and Lil, a single nurse came to our house whenever they were around. Lil was mostly an up-country nurse. Bob was wherever needed. After a while, they came together and were always welcomed.

The kids and I loved their company. And then came Bob and Lil's wedding. Wayne and Lydia Halliday played mom and dad and Zeke and I were attendants. Lynette got to be flower girl. They were married in the Addis church on a Sunday afternoon. The only real family in attendance was Lil's cousin who flew in from Moshi, Tanzania. Everyone came to our house for the reception. We had about fifty or more for that really special dinner. Roasted pig with an apple in its mouth and all the trimmings. Since we overlooked the crater lake, we borrowed card tables and chairs and seated everyone outside. It was a beautiful afternoon. The builder was a Norwegian with a wife and eight children. What a surprise when they arrived and his wife asked for table space and came in carrying a huge mirror. "Now what do I do with that wedding cake we had made so special?" I had used cake mixes that I had baked and frozen. Then a special house boy from Addis came and created a very beautiful wedding cake. The cake was beautiful. We also made homemade ice cream. We had Norwegian goodies, like cream puffs and eclairs. They needed to be spread out. That's what the Norwegians do for weddings. Surprised, but it worked out great. We were all pleased with the very special wedding celebration.

We also went camping with the mission group and Zeke made it a hunting trip. That was a memorable weekend. There must have been six or more families. We arrived late afternoon and got our tent setup. All was going well until a storm came. The wind blew hard, and it rained. Didn't have a tornado, but we had really strong winds. Being in it was not fun. Then someone else arrived. It was already dark. Zeke went to help them setup. Meanwhile the kids and I were fighting the tent, trying to keep it from blowing away. Next day, it was calm. We had survived the storm.

Late that afternoon, the men went hunting for lion and then came upon a large male. Zeke was waiting to get a perfect shot. He was the hunter and the plan was that no one else would shoot, only for emergency. He fumed, was really upset, when the doctor fired before he did. Not only killing the lion but ripping the hide so it could not be salvaged. I still have the claw made up into a pendant. One less skin to have mounted.

The real reason Zeke wanted to go to Africa was to hunt. He did a lot of it. Not all for trophies. Some was for food. We ate lots of antelope meat. It was so much better than beef. Animals living in the wild went where there was water and food, nutrients tamed animals lacked. They never got big or fat. Often the trip to the market caused them to lose many pounds.

Animals made it dangerous to drive at night. You could not see them on the road unless you were facing them. We did not like going home from Addis on Sunday nights for that reason. Their eyes sparkled in the headlights if you are facing them but you don't get much when you see the tail. Mostly, it was cattle on the roads on the way to Monday morning market. Cattle were very skinny, huge horns, spread wide. We had a set of horns above our arch which was six feet wide. Zeke had scraped them, sanded, and made them smooth. He loved those horns. What a stinky mess when he was doing that! Not as bad as the rotten ostrich egg that he brought home. The guys at the farm really liked it when Zeke went out, shot food for the workers at the farm after a big holiday and fasting over. One time he shot a zebra for food, strictly as last resort as nothing was available. Most of the time it was kudu, gazelle, impala, or even wild pig. I had an electric roaster. Many times, for company I cooked a whole hind quarter of any of the above. Always a treat for company.

We loved the beautiful birds and had quite a collection mounted. We brought them back to the states. Especially Steve liked the bird books and learned to know them by name. I particularly liked the carmine bee-eater, the rollers, hoopies and flycatcher. Mostly, we watched the sunbirds around the lantana while sitting in the front yard, under the grape arbor. They fluttered much like hummingbirds. Lots of bugs, especially colorful moths. We had beautiful flowers. Poinsetta in the backyard, like a tree. It bloomed at Christmas time. I had brought dahlia bulbs. Everone liked them. I had them out back with the banana trees. Our bananas were very small, pinkish inside and tasted a bit more like strawberries. Kids loved the papayas from our trees. We ate many of them. My favorite was custard apples. I haven't tasted them again.

Camping trips were not always fun, just too much effort. If we didn't go to a lake, had to take water for washing up, and required plenty of drinking water since it needed to be boiled. By the time I had the hassle of three kids, all the gears set, it wasn't worth it. Most of the camping trips proved to be hunting trips.

I really enjoyed going to Lake Langano, where they had cabins and served meals. That was my idea of camping. They always served fresh caught fish for dinner, and that was special. The country side going to one of the lakes was much the same, wide open spaces, not much growth, and villages few and far between. Anytime you stopped along the road, someone always showed up in five or ten minutes. Always had to rush our potty stops. We knew we didn't have much time. Seldom had a hiding place either. Probably the biggest and best place would be a huge ant hill. Lots of termites that made huge mounds, and underneath would be the queen. One could never destroy the hill without doing away with the queen. Kids loved the ant hills as they were fun to climb. It was fun to climb. Lots of sights along the way, you could find all sort of things to buy. Snake skins were a popular sale. They could be huge. Beggars always wanted cans, *koro*. We always kept empty cans in the car to give away. It really was hard to get accustomed to so many beggars everyplace we went.

The last trip to Lake Langano, I went with the Hallidays, and their water resources friends. Zeke was off on a hunting trip. I came to the realization I was eating everything that didn't eat me.

When the kids and I got back home I realized I was pregnant. What a shocker. We would be going back to the states in about two months.

That hunting trip was at least a week. Zeke and three of his friends took two jeeps, went south of Addis into pretty much untraveled country. They had planned this safari for several months. Chief of the safari was Haile Selassie's right hand mechanic. He was in charge of Haile Selassie's personal plane and also associated with Ethiopian airlines. He was a special mechanic. We heard nothing from them until they returned. It was one hectic of a trip. The rain came They brought back pictures of what the roads looked like. Aunt Emma had commented on the picture, "And you called that a vacation." Anyway, it even got too rough for those four, tough, and determined hunters. When they got far enough south to make contact in Addis, they had a plane come to pick up the jeeps and the hunters and bring them back home. No trophies.

Our tour was for two years but we decided to stay on an additional six months and not return. Mostly wanted to go someplace where Steve could go to school and the kids and I would not be so isolated. The guys had a great party for us just before we left and asked us to invite one couple to join us. Our best friends, the Hedricks joined us so it was thirteen guys and the new secretary. She had done much of the cooking and arranging. We had a huge spread of Ethiopian food that all of us had learned to love. I made them promise me that they would not make me eat raw meat. They had a special ceremonial cake too. They gave me a silver charm bracelet and fabric for their style of dress. The fabric was always white and thin, a very course weave. Borders were colorful and the wider the border, the more expensive the fabric. Mine was a beautiful dark red. Tears were shed when we left Ethiopia as it was such a wonderful experience. I learned really a lot about life and sometimes it was very rewarding to watch people laughing and having so much fun when they had so little.

* * *

Today, in 2017, after twenty-five years I have taken these pages out of the drawer. At first, I said, *ishe, nega*, meaning okay tomorrow, and then tomorrow never came so life went on and I forgot about writing. Sometimes, it was just better to live in the present. I was having plenty of problems doing that. Steve just had his 61st birthday and he was five when we took that long trip to Africa. Many times, he has said he would like to go back home. We did go back with West Virginia University and lived two years in both Tanzania and Uganda. Later lived in Iran for four years.

It was difficult for us to adjust to state side living after being gone so long. The kids had always gone to very small schools so how do they adjust when being tossed into such drastic change. Steve finished the last two years of high school. When he graduated it was a class of one thousand. In his freshman and sophomore years of high school, he went to a small French speaking boarding school in Switzerland. Monte had his first year at home with me and correspondence school. Instead of going back to Montana we stayed in Oklahoma City as Zeke had a short time job with World Bank. Adjustment to life was as difficult coming back here as it was going overseas.

I had a very interesting experience a few years ago after sister-in-law told me she had just read a book that she really enjoyed and thought I would also. I got it at the library, *Three Cups of Tea* by Greg Mortenson. On page eight, I read that his mother's name was Jerene. Now how many people are named Jerene? This was the Jerene who came for Bob and Lil's wedding. I was already getting chills when he talked about Moshi and Tanzania. That brought about my calling Bob and Lil. Wonderful to reminisce and learn about their family. Later I went to Norman, Oklahoma University when Greg Mortenson came to give a talk and signed his books. He signed his second book, *Stones into Schools*. He was just a little boy when we went to their house in Moshi and borrowed a basket for my new baby to sleep in. I had contacted Jerene in Moshi as we were

in Arusha, Tanzania for six weeks. My baby LeAnn was only seven weeks old and she had been sleeping in a box. When we returned to the states from Ethiopia we left again as soon as she was four weeks old.

I have done some checking on the Lutheran mission that was started in 1959, just before we got there in 1961. In the '70s, there was a lot of change that took place but that original mission grew and grew, and at the present time it is still called Mekane Yesus. It has a membership of over eight million. It is made up of 8500 congregation with 4000 preaching stations. Ethiopia always had many Orthodox Christians.

It seemed I remembered that Princess Aida and Sophia had gone to Europe when the major problems came about in the mid '70s and Haile Selasie died or was murdered. However, I have just read a whole different ending and came as such a sad situation. The ladies of the royal family were all put in a prison at that time, including the mother Tenagnawork, Aida, and Sophia. Fourteen years in confinement, sleeping on the floor on a mattress, with one light bulb in the one big room that burned twenty-four hours a day. Many of men in the family were put to death and one of the sisters took her own life. Grandsons were also imprisoned. Aida died several years ago and the mother passed some years back. I still regret that I did not follow up and go to the palace.

I also read that the "hyena man" was still doing his thing. Sounds as if they are making even much more of a theatric production out of it now.

Sometimes I think of that house, up from the lake, with all its windows and scenic and wonder. Did we really live in Ethiopia, so very, very far away? We watched the birds, moths, and the animals. The kids were so young. They don't remember that much. LeAnn, you were there, but you didn't get to see out. I try to remember the amharic words, and counting but it has slipped away throughout the many years. That was a very "whatever" kind of life. As a child, I loved the books by Oza and Harriet Johnson that I got from the school library. Loved the stories about Africa and never dreamed that one day I would be able to speak about Africa and tell stories myself.

* * *

Now, we would be without a home, or a job and another baby on the way. Our household furnishings were in storage in Montana. We needed an address to receive airfreight and sea freight from overseas.

When we'd left Bozeman, Montana, Zeke had anticipated returning to the old job, and being away treated as a sabbatical. However, there were forced layoffs. Employed only two year with Oklahoma State, Zeke was the first to receive a pink slip. No job when we got back to the states.

West Virginia had a contract with Tanzania, Uganda, and US government, same as Oklahoma State had had with Ethiopia. We'd hoped we could return to one of those countries. We contacted West Virginia to seek employment in either of the above countries. Strictly, this was a wait and see. Our plan was to go to California and Oklahoma and back to Montana—wait out the new baby. Hopefully after that we would have a job someplace. It was a stressful time but what choice did we have?

The game parks of Tanzania and Uganda were neighbors to Ethiopia. If we could return to Africa after the new baby came we would have the opportunity to do this, but that might not have been an option.

Decision was made to take a side trip on the way to the United States and visit four of the game parks now. We had to take advantage of the opportunity or it might be the regret of our lives.

I had been to Nairobi with two of my gal friends on a four-day shopping trip and it was so much fun. No one goes to Nairobi, now or ever, without going to the New Stanley Hotel and the Thorn Tree restaurant. Those two places will live on forever as they are the history of Nairobi and its growth. We did a lot of girl things. *I was pretty bitchy when I got back as I had just returned from a visit in heaven. Back to reality.*

Our tour was over in July and that ended our six-month extension.

Nairobi would be our destination. From there we would go to Serengeti, on to the Ngorongoro Crater, and then to Manyara. It was a good time to go. The rains would be over and the wildebeest migration still occurring. The terrain would be very different since that whole area had been changed by craters millions of years before.

Nairobi National Park is only four miles south of the city, 29,000 acres, comparatively small. It was established as a park in 1946. The town was growing and animals were causing the people significant problems. People were not able to grow crops, be safe in their houses as the animals just roamed the area. Interesting to read *Circling the Sun* by Paula McLain. She writes about Nairobi in the 1920's. An electric fence was built around three sides of the designated park area. There is a river on the south side and farther south is a conservation area which helps animals' migration. The terrain is varied. Some places are high and steep and extends north to the Kenya border, where this park is mostly flat grassland and quite dry. The river to the south provides water for the animals.

Wonderful to go to Nairobi and see such a variety of animals. It has become a sanctuary for rhinoceroses, seen in all of the parks. We saw many of the basic animals—zebras, giraffes, lions, gazelles, etc. and strange that they could be so close to a large city. Only place where you could be looking at a tall giraffe, and in the background, see Nairobi's skyscrapers.

The kids were very impressed with Whimpey's. They had a burger and fries. Of course they were too young to realize what a burger was to an American. They saw many different things in Nairobi. Living as we did, they had had a sheltered life, and here saw things they had never seen before—even sidewalks. We had to be careful not to fall off while looking at the tall buildings. It was an exceptionally beautiful city. The main streets were filled with bougainvillea that bloomed profusely.

I needed to proceed with caution with weight gain while in that pregnant state. The food was amazing. Really a mix of many nationalities and heard an assortment of languages.

Off to the Serengeti Plains in our rented Land Rover, heading south, and west to Tanzania. Beautiful scenic country—green hills and coffee plantations. Lots of birds and we saw animals along the way. The varied terrain, said by scientists, was the result of many volcano activity that shaped the plain, added mountains and craters, and formed the Serengeti.

This was our first time to cross the equator and it was hot. Animals had problems surviving due to everything drying up quickly. Many needed to migrate to survive. Rainy season was March and May and then again in November and December. As it dried up, food not available, more than a million wildebeests begin to go northeast in the park that took them to the Kenya border. The travel was so difficult that 250,000 would die along the way. Babies were only a month or two old.
Being tired and weak, many animals died trying to cross the river. Zebras followed and many gazelles too.

If you put your head down to the ground, you could hear, and feel, the impact of the hoofs. Then came the predators, waiting for one to fall, and easily have a feast. Animals returned south again in November when the rain came again. Mostly a 500-mile trip going from one end of the plains to the other.

Loved the animals! We saw so many different species. Lots of wildebeests, zebras and gazelles of course. Lions, leopards, and cheetahs were beautiful. Impalas, amazingly graceful when running. The waterbucks were chunky, stately, and one of my favorites. Giraffes were majestic in the wild. When you are close to them it seemed, they could just step right over you.

Serengeti is 12,000 square miles of endless plains and you did not have to drive far to see something.

In 1950, Bernhard Grzimek, and his son Michael, produced a film and book titled *Serengeti Shall Not Die* as there had been so much killing and poaching of animals. He wanted to save the animals. People were destroying the lion population.

Originally, various tribes populated the area, especially the Maasai warriors, a colorful and interesting group, living all over Tanzania, and also, in Kenya. They were not permitted to live in Serengeti. They survived with their herds of cattle, their form of wealth, that provided meat and milk. They also drank the blood of the animals. Men carried spears and used shields. Literally colorful. They painted their bodies with red color. Great to watch them as a group, running and chanting in beaded clothes and red skin, carrying shields.

We stayed at a lodge where we had a cabin, only a bar where guests assembled at dusk to discuss the day's find. The parks had strict rules. They didn't want anyone out after sunset. We had fun meeting a filming crew, from St. Louis, doing a series of animal shows for children TV. They would meet William Holden when they got back to Nairobi. They invited us to join them next evening at Ngorongoro Crater.

Back to our cabin where our cook had dinner ready. We brought our own food and a cook would prepare it for us. There were no restaurant services available. No, we did not have an ice chest loaded with goodies! It was a dinner of canned meat, canned beans, and a can of peaches for dessert. We were on safari and it was great at Serengeti. Trip of a lifetime! Tomorrow, we would move on.

It was a two to three-hour drive to the Ngorongoro Crater, the largest one in the world. Trip started out leaving the plains on a wide and flat dusty road going southeast that changed to a narrow, winding, and slicky, wet road. We thought the rain was over but not there. We saw signs that said, "Watch for the elephants."

About that time, the Land Rover went into a skid and we did a 360-degree turnabout. There weren't any elephants on the road but we certainly saw signs that they had been there. Lots of tree damage.

An amazing view looking down into the crater, unbelievable sight as that was an area of about one hundred square miles and two thousand feet down to the crater floor. It was a slow, winding descent to the crater's floor.

There were no giraffes or impalas but we saw plenty of other animals. Hippos and rhinos were there. We had not seen any in the other parks. They were huge! As difficult as it may seem, a few of these animals do migrate. I've read that the lions of Ngorongoro would not permit other lions to come in their park.

The Maasai nomads were permitted to live and herd their cattle there. Many had come from Serengeti when they were forced out of that park. Food and water were not easy to come by. However, they could survive on their cattle. You never saw them without their swords, spears, and colorful dress. They liked piercing their ears and did much stretching of the earlobes. In full dress, such as police officers, dress uniform was with "ears tucked." (The extended piercing was tucked up and over the top of the ear).

After the wide-open spaces of Serengeti and the ten-mile wide, twelve-mile long crater floor, it was time to move on to Manyara Park.

Once again, the road took us farther southeast to a much different terrain. The park was about the same size as Ngorongoro, a bit larger, maybe. At least half of its 127-square miles was water. Trees and more trees and even palm trees, but mostly acacias and baobobs. The story was that when God made the baobab tree, he was not happy with it, so he pulled it back up, and turned it over, and planted it again, this time with the roots sticking up and above. The lions loved the acacia trees. Looking overhead into the acacia trees it was not unusual to see one or more lions sleeping.

Since there was so much more rain and water, there was not much tree destruction. Since the elephant population was the chief destroyer of trees, here there was more food available.

Africa, known for its beautiful birds, there was paradise for them. Many flamingos and other water birds. Great park to go to if you just want to bird watch.

That was the only park where we saw leopards, so special, sleek, and gorgeous. We had seen cheetahs. They don't have those special spots like the leopards. Cheetahs, like lions, like to sleep in acacia trees.

The giraffes were happy there. They loved the little acacia leaves they could reach, get their small mouths between the big thorns, and get those tasty foliage. It was fun watching giraffes in the wild and their graceful movements. *Which was longer, the legs or the neck? How much effort does it take to reach the top or the bottom?* Fascinating animals! I never grew tired of watching them as they had so far to reach and did it with such ease and elegance.

Lots of elephants there and enough food for them. They could hide easily among the trees. We came up on one bull elephant in a clearing. He did not like us invading his territory. Kids and I thought it was plain frightening when he lifted its trunk and trumpeted while running toward us. Our driver did a quick turn about and the elephant turned around too. At times, we had to wait for elephants and giraffes to get out of the road. We did not see tree damage in that park as we did in others since there was more vegetation for the masses of animals.

We met the St Louis filming crew both at Ngorongoro, and again, at Manyara. It was like seeing old friends. The lodge and restaurant were very nice. We really enjoyed our stay at that place.

Now it was time to return to the Land Rover. Back to Arusha and then north to Nairobi. That weeklong trip was one special experience and too bad the kids were too young to remember.

We took the polar route back to the United States, flew over Iceland, Greenland, and landed in California to spend time with the Thies family. That was a very long flight. The kids were real troopers and I was proud to be traveling with them. They realized they were living a special life. It was emotional for me when the plane touched down on American soil. There is just nothing like "coming home."

~ Ethiopia photographs from the 1960s ~

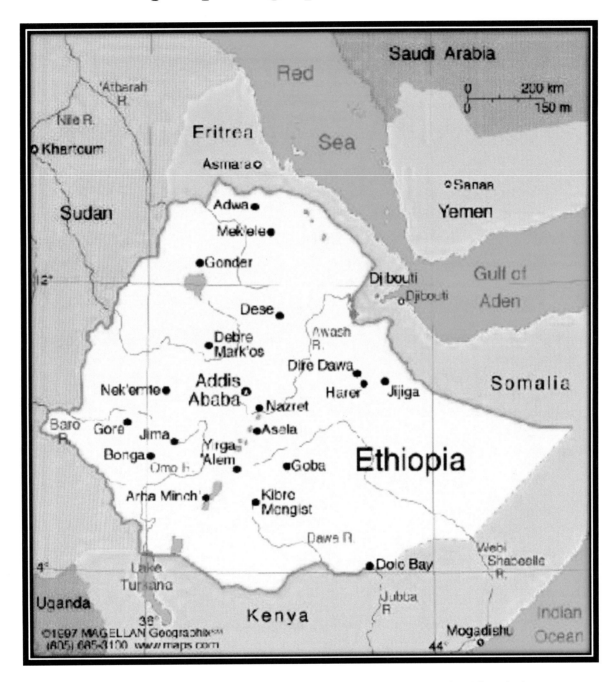

Bishoftu/Debra Zeit is about 50 kilometer (30 miles) southeast of Addis Ababa.
The High School was in Jima to the east. The college was at Dire Dawa with
Hyena Man near Harar to the northeast.

Ethiopian Flag

Steve, Monte, and Lynette at home in Bozeman, Montana.

Washington D.C. - Getting ready for Kennedy Inauguration.

Greece - Sissy in the bus sleeping while we enjoy the sights.

Bishoftu/Debra Zeit, the farm, and our purpose for being in Ethiopia.

Town's main street. Everyone home for afternoon rest.

Farmers met at the farm to learn new methods.

Trial plots to determine best varieties for weather conditions and resistance to disease.

Farm was to help make life easier and more productive.

Few people owned horses as they were used in celebrations. Oxen were much more practical for farm usage.

A   B   C

A: Like bible times, separating grain from the chaff.
B: Big haystack made with only manpower.
C: Building a chicken house – incubators & eggs would arrive from the states soon so an American variety of plumb chickens would be introduced.

Our house on crater lake, beautiful view, big backyard, but not walled, or gated.

A

B

C

D

A: Now how is that for a turtle! It roamed the area for about a week befor moving away.
B: Poinsettias prettiest in December - also had banana and papaya trees in the backyard.
C: Big pool that did not hold water but was fun. At one time, it was about half full, and great, as we had no water in the house for a few days.
D: Our house in Debra Zeit – Sliding doors and big windows made for scenic view of crater lake below. Lots of tea parties under the grape arbor using wicker chairs and table.

My two favorite hunters: Monte and Lynette.

Finally, got the Opel. Check the open window – neighbor's monkey came in a few times as there were no screens and not possible to have some.

Street scenes of Addis Abba.

Bridge built by the Italians.

Lion of Judah Monument.

A monument in a traffic circle.

Coptic Christian churches and scenes near Addis.

Security walls were around many buildings.

Orthodox Christian Church

Modern office building. Traffic circles were used as they had very few lights.

Road to Jima: Tukels constructed to tolerate rain and weather conditions.

Only thing missing would be windows. Thatch all the way to the ground was seldom seen.

Natives lived close together for protection from animals.

Steep sloped roofs to cope with frequent heavy rain.

Lories and cattle can be a real problem on roads.

Would you want a roof over your head? Natives carrying a new roof to the tukel.

It might be a week or more before
this accident is cleared.

Legs and heads were all you could see
after they finished loading the donkey.

The natives liked when the locusts came. They were a delicacy.

Work for the women and girls was never finished as most of them even needed to transport water in pots carried on their heads.

Plenty of wood in this area.

No washboard – easier to take clothes to the water.

Crowds gathered instantly. No bathrooms when traveling – so make a quick stop.

Carrying cow dung – used as main source for heat.

More jobs every day

Herding cattle, but time out to pose – they loved pictures.

Two mini herders.

A little family time while watching the lentils dry – starting to weave on the right side.

A

B

C

A: Horse ready for celebration. Rider would be dressed in white but also have colorful attire and carry a fly switcher. That was a decorative handle with horse tail hair so the rider could casually flip away the flies.

B: This was an amazing mud construction as it had windows. Elongated structure with thatched roof and beautiful. Built on a sugar plantation.

C: Also on the sugar plantation – operated by Europeans with irrigation water so area was beautiful with flowers.

Kids loved climbing ant hills.

A

B

C

A: These Gala girls were always ready to sell some beads.
B: Negotiating the price of a bracelet - money, not cans.
C: They were so ready to have picture made but wanted some tin cans (korokoro) in return.

Memorials are found most anyplace. All of these were near the roads as we were going to one of the lakes. This was constructed for someone very special as it required a lot of effort. Collecting and bringing in the rock and then much carving.

Sometimes, memorials were crude. Animal horns were attached to the sticks. Crude, but special.

This one, probably for a specific tribal leader. But very elegant to be found in this location.

Looks like she really had a fun time!

We did have fish for dinner as the European lodge owner always served fresh caught fish from the lake. Was such a treat for the kids and myself when we could go to the lake and stay at a lodge.

Don't know where we are going to play ball!

Come on Dad, let's go!

Just beautiful memories.

Acacia trees (picture used on book cover) were very common - made a beautiful umbrella.

Crater lake just below our house. Hotel and emperor's weekend home were just across the lake.

Debra Zeit Market

Mercato in Addis was more fun. It went on & on. But pictures were not allowed.
Head gear helps keep flies away and cooler too.

A

B

A: Fabric was very thin. Much like our cheese cloth. Borders were woven and very colorful.
Wider was always more expensive.
B: Debra Zeit Market.

Hunting Trip – South of Addis

Very special bridge built by the Italians.
Not all bridges were like this.

They didn't have money for clothes and
was not always available.

Countryside going far south, near the Kenya border.

More hunting.

There's a bridge but it's safer through the river.

A

B

A: They called this a vacation!
B: It took about a week to get to their destination. About an hour flight to get back to Addis on the Ethiopian Airline.

In Memoriam

Siegbert (Zeke) A. Thies
August 10, 1928
February 23, 1988

~

~

- Equator -
~ Game Parks Photographs ~
Tanzania, Kenya

Serengeti - Tanzania
~ Hot and dry – mostly plains ~

The Sausage Tree – but don't eat them!

Wildebeeste migration: Also known as gnu, they travel north and west from April through October/November looking for fresh grass. Many zebras and gazelles go with them. Babies are born in February so many die on this long journey, many predators, and at the end of the trip is a fierce river to cross.

Giraffe

Ostrich

With their long legs and long necks they are fun characters to watch.

Lion

Topi

Thompson Gazelle

Hartebeest

Zebra

Ngorongoro Crater - Tanzania
~ 10 miles wide, 12 miles long, and about 1/3-mile deep ~
Largest crater in the world.

Rhino

Oryx

Waterbuck

Waterbuck

Impala

Night time visit from the hyena man as he is calling the hyenas in by clattering bones.

Hyena   Wild Dog

Zebra - Oryx

Tree damage due to too many elephants.

Maasai

Maasai tribe was moved out of Serengeti but Ngorongoro let them come into the crater with their cattle. They were not permitted to live there. They are nomads and warriors and very interesting people.

Mound Homes

Manyara – Tanzania
~ Nearly half of the area is lake ~

Elephant

Lion

Lion

Leopard
Settled in for a good night's sleep.

Cheetah at dusk - enjoying the view.

Buffalo

Warthog: Ugly but very good to eat. They grow to be a good size animal and were smart enough to go where they could find food.

Lizard – a very common sight.

Flamingo

Bee Eater

Roller

Kingfisher

Crested Crane

Family

LeAnn was born November 11, 1963, and we would be going back to Tanzania.

We flew from Bozeman to California, December 11th. LeAnn was introduced to family in California, then to Oklahoma for Christmas, and spent New Year's Eve in Morgantown, West Virginia. Forced to stay there for a full week as LeAnn's passport had not caught up with us in Oklahoma.

After a few days in Athens, we went on to Dar es Salaam. The kids and I were in a guest house while Zeke, my husband, went on to language school in Arusha, the land of game parks. After three days, I insisted we go to Arusha for the six weeks of language school, or the kids and I would return to the states.

While in Arusha, we visited Tsavo Park before going on to Morogoro for two years. Since we were the first and only Americans there from West Virginia, not just in Morogoro, but in Tanzania, it was an extraordinary stay. For three or four months, we slept on cornhusk mattresses. We lived off the local market and did not have contact with other Americans until West Virginia sent others to complete our group.

About the Author

Arlene (Wiersig) Thies was born in a farmhouse on a cold and windy day, March 5, 1931, in Alva, Oklahoma, with doctor Daniel Ensor in attendance. She lived with the fun of an icebox, a cistern, and an outhouse, but blessed to have had electricity.

She attended a two-room parochial grade school for eight years which taught reading, writing, and arithmetic. 4-H club was introduced where she learned cooking, gardening, canning, sewing, and healthy living.

Arlene graduated from Alva High School in 1948. Then she graduated from St. John's two-year college in Winfield, Kansas. Her attendance at St. John's was a highlight time for her where she learned to have fun, laugh, and play.

She taught four grades with thirty-four children in a two-room parochial school in Freeman South Dakota, earning one-hundred-fifty dollars a month. Also, taught in Perryville, Missouri, and Ft. Smith, Arkansas.

Married, she lived in Sidney and Bozeman, Montana, before going to Ethiopia, Tanzania, Uganda, and Iran.

Arlene moved back to Oklahoma in 1975 so that her four children could attend stateside schools and experience the American life.

She divorced in 1978.

After working at many different jobs, Arlene settled at Oklahoma Gas and Electric and retired from there in year 2000 and now lives in Oklahoma City, Oklahoma.

68995416R10049

Made in the USA
Lexington, KY
23 October 2017